50 POISONOUS QUESTIONS

A BOOK WITH BITE

TANYA
LLOYD KYI

ILLUSTRATED BY
ROSS KINNAIRD

annick press
toronto + new york + vancouver

This book is the second in the 50 Questions series.
Text © 2011 Tanya Lloyd Kyi
Illustrations © 2011 Ross Kinnaird

ANNICK PRESS LTD.

Edited by Catherine Marjoribanks
Copyedited by Elizabeth McLean
Cover and interior design by Irvin Cheung / iCheung Design, inc.
Cover illustration by Ross Kinnaird
oil barrel image: © istockphoto.com / Valerie Loiseleux

We acknowledge the support of the Canada Council for the Arts, the Ontario Arts Council, and the Government of Canada through the Canada Book Fund (CBF) for our publishing activities.

 ONTARIO ARTS COUNCIL
CONSEIL DES ARTS DE L'ONTARIO

CATALOGING IN PUBLICATION
Kyi, Tanya Lloyd, 1973-
    50 poisonous questions : a book with bite / Tanya Lloyd Kyi ; illustrated by Ross Kinnaird.

(50 questions series)
Includes bibliographical references and index.
ISBN 978-1-55451-281-2 (bound).—ISBN 978-1-55451-280-5 (pbk.)

    1. Poisons—Juvenile literature. I. Kinnaird, Ross, 1954- II. Title. III. Title: Fifty poisonous questions. IV. Series: 50 Questions series ; 2

RA1214.K95 2011   j615.9   C2010-906868-8

Printed and bound in China

Published in the U.S.A. by
Annick Press (U.S.) Ltd.

Distributed in Canada by
Firefly Books Ltd.
66 Leek Crescent
Richmond Hill, ON
L4B 1H1

Distributed in the U.S.A. by
Firefly Books (U.S.) Inc.
P.O. Box 1338
Ellicott Station
Buffalo, NY 14205

Visit our website at **www.annickpress.com**

Visit Tanya Lloyd Kyi at **www.tanyalloydkyi.com**

To Julia
— T.K.

For Hannah
— R.K.

Acknowledgments

A big thank you to Catherine Marjoribanks and Elizabeth McLean for guiding this book, and to Irvin Cheung for a design which exploits all its poisonous possibilities.

TABLE OF CONTENTS

start Here!

CAUTION: BIOHAZARD!

STOP! DO NOT, UNDER ANY CIRCUMSTANCES, EAT THIS BOOK. Do not drink it. Do not touch it without the protection of latex gloves. Every single page is coated in poison. Unidentified noxious substances might drip from the spine at any time, and the fumes have yet to be tested in reliable laboratories. While reading some chapters, you may want to hold your breath.

The poisons contained here range from the venom of the tiniest ant to the toxic waste of the largest factories. There are spider bites, jellyfish tentacles, scorpion tails, berries, weeds, leaves, rocks, gases, lakes, clouds, chemical corporations, and ocean bays. For safety reasons, oceans should probably be avoided altogether.

DO NOT FEED (OR TOUCH) THE ANIMALS.

DO NOT

USE THE RECIPES.

DO NOT

KISS THE GOLDEN DART FROGS.

Should you choose to continue reading, slip on a lab coat. Invest in good protective eyewear. And step into the world of ancient alchemists and modern scientists, those who delve into the mysteries of Earth's most murderous chemicals.

You have been warned.

DO NOT

FOLLOW THE ADVICE IN THIS BOOK.

Chapter 1

SPIKES & FANGS

I hate witches!

Eye of newt and toe of frog—that's what you need for a witches' brew. But are frogs really poisonous? And how noxious is a newt? What most of us know about venomous snakes, amphibians, and sea creatures is a mixture of fact and fiction. Some of it comes from textbooks and some comes from scary stories and superstitions.

In reality, a *poison* is a substance that's harmful when eaten, breathed, or absorbed. *Venom* is a poison that's injected—as in, through a snake's fangs. And *toxin* is another name for a poison produced by a living thing. The questions in this chapter help sort the real toxins from the tall tales.

What has the fiercest fangs?

SLIPPERY AND SLITHERING, maws dripping with venom, snakes have wound their way into horror movies and nightmares. Not many of them deserve this frightening reputation. There are almost 3000 species of snakes in the world and many of them *do* have poisonous saliva. But a snake needs two things to be considered venomous—a toxin, and a way to inject it.

It needs fangs!

Only about 500 species have teeth long and sharp enough to effectively poison their prey. The most toxic of these is the beaked sea snake, a brown-patterned water-dweller the length of a skipping rope. With its specially adapted lungs and nostrils, the serpent can remain underwater for up to eight hours, feasting on fish. But when threatened by a predator, it can easily turn aggressive.

On land, the world's most venomous snake is the inland taipan of Australia. It injects enough poison in one bite to kill 100 people.

Neither of these snakes is responsible for many human deaths. That's because there aren't a lot of people swimming the Indian Ocean or hiking the Australian outback. Most of the 30,000 to 40,000 people killed by snakes each year live in rural areas of the tropics, in developing countries where people walk barefoot and the nearest medical clinic might be hours away.

She bit her tongue.

FANG FLAVORS

Snake venom is a combination of proteins and enzymes—a kind of super-saliva that starts dissolving prey on contact. The three main varieties of venom have scientific names that give you a clue to understanding what makes them so dangerous. For starters, the word "toxic" refers to a poisonous substance produced by living cells or organisms. Since *hemo* is the Greek word for "blood," a hemotoxic venom is one that affects the blood; *neuro* means "nerve," so a neurotoxic venom affects the nervous system, causing breathing problems and paralysis (not to mention excruciating pain); and *cyto* means cell, so a *cytotoxic* venom affects only the cells in the area of the bite.

56 Flavors

Foul Fact
Even in Australia, with more than 60 poisonous species of snake, only a few people die each year from snake bites. People are more likely to be killed by lightning.

Can sheep cure snake bites?

WHEN YOU GO TO THE HEALTH CLINIC for a vaccine, a nurse will inject a small amount of an actual disease under your skin. There's not enough of the virus to make you sick, just enough to make your body's natural defenses against illness spring into action. Once the vaccine has taught your immune system to fight off the bug, you're protected from the illness in the future.

Antivenins are treatments for venomous snake bites that work in much the same way. Instead of giving a human a small dose of snake venom, however, researchers inject an animal—often a sheep. They allow the animal's immune system to react and learn to fight the venom's effects. Then, workers draw blood samples from the animal and use them to make the antivenin. When the antivenin is administered to a person who has been bitten by a venomous snake, it neutralizes the venom so it can't do any further harm.

Sounds simple, right? There are a few problems. First, turning animal blood into human medicine is a long and expensive process. Treating one patient with a North American rattlesnake antivenin can cost $20,000. Clinics in many countries can't afford to keep antivenin on hand. Another problem: antivenin itself can be toxic, and snakes don't record how much venom they inject. What if doctors use too much antivenin? What if the bite was from a poisonous snake, but it didn't inject venom? What if the victim says it was a cobra, but it was actually a krait? In those cases, the treatment can be more dangerous than the bite.

7

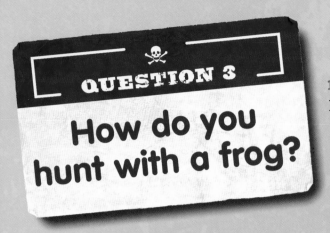

QUESTION 3

How do you hunt with a frog?

1. **HEAD TO COLOMBIA** and catch a large batch of golden dart frogs. These tiny yellow-orange frogs are the size of daisies and just as innocent-looking. But they snack on noxious insects, which have munched on poisonous plants.

2. Boil the whole frogs until you've created a thick, poisonous stew. Or, if you only need one or two poison darts, simply rub the tip of your weapon on the back of a sweaty frog.

3. As the native people of the region have done for thousands of years, load your darts into a blowpipe. Be careful not to touch them with your bare hands.

4. Blow a dart at the animal of your choice. There's enough poison in one frog to kill more than 10 people, making the golden dart frog the world's most toxic vertebrate. Your dart will kill a monkey in only a moment or two. Even a jaguar will only last a few minutes.

Foul Fact

Snake handlers in Thailand chew the root of the turmeric plant, which apparently makes them more resistant to cobra venom.

UNNERVING NEWTS

If you went to the dentist for a filling, you'd receive a local anesthetic. This type of medicine puts your pain nerves on hold by blocking something in the nerve called the sodium channel. Different creatures have different types of nervous systems, but they all have sodium channels. And it turns out that newts knew about sodium channels long before doctors and dentists. A newt's poison can block all sodium channels and cause paralysis—or death, if the newt is eaten by a hungry snake or bird. Some bugs, frogs, and scorpions use the same kind of poison.

This won't hurt a bit.

THE KOMODO DRAGON OF INDONESIA could use better dental care. It feeds on dead animals, and it gets bits of flesh stuck between its teeth. For years, scientists believed that it was these pieces of germy meat that made the komodo's bite dangerous.

Only in the last decade have researchers discovered poison in the creature's saliva. And they've learned that other lizards are venomous as well. It seems that 60 million years ago, lizards and venomous snakes shared the same great-great-great-great... grandparents.

For the komodo dragon, the combination of venom and bacteria from the rotting bits of food is perfect for hunting. The lizard can bite an animal as big as a water buffalo and then retreat to the reeds and wait a few days, until the animal succumbs to infection. Then it's dinnertime!

QUESTION 4

Is there carrion on the menu?

10

SPINES AND SNAILS AND STINGRAY TAILS

From miniature blue-ringed octopuses with lethal bites to venom-equipped stingrays the size of baby elephants, the oceans are teeming with toxins. Scientists have counted 1,200 poisonous fish species. One of the most dangerous lurks in underwater sand, its warts and wrinkles blending almost perfectly with the mottled surface. When the sneaky stonefish gulps down smaller fish for dinner, 13 spines along its back protect it from attack. If a shark noses the stonefish, the spines project deadly venom.

There are probably more poisonous underwater species yet to be discovered. In 2009, deep in an underwater lava tube off the Canary Islands, divers found a tiny, toxic crustacean no one had ever seen before. It had no eyes—only searching antennae and vicious fangs.

Yikes! Get me outta here!

11

QUESTION 5

Do snails carry weapons?

THE CONE SNAIL DOESN'T HAVE TEETH—it has hollow, barbed darts filled with venom. When a fish swims by, the snail wraps its proboscis, or snout, around a dart. Then it plucks the weapon from its mouth and stabs its prey. The tooth itself can be tossed away—there are 20 more in different growth stages inside the snail.

Since the cone snail is too small and slow to chase after a dying fish, its venom must be powerful enough to paralyze instantly. Scientists are particularly interested in the substance, partly because it contains almost 100 distinct poisons—and because the victims of the snail don't seem to feel pain as they die. The venom contains a powerful painkiller, which might someday be useful to human medicine.

ON A LIST OF DANGEROUS OCEAN CREATURES, you might rank a shark higher than a jellyfish. But what if the jellyfish was the size of a basketball, and had tentacles loaded with thousands of poison darts, just waiting for a fish or a surfer to brush past?

The sea wasp jellyfish is the most dangerous ocean-dweller around. Its toxin is designed to instantly paralyze its prey. That way, the jellyfish can eat at a leisurely pace, with no danger to its gelatinous curves.

Contrary to popular belief, you're not supposed to pee on a jellyfish sting. The best cure—other than antivenin—is to douse the wound in vinegar. This helps to neutralize the poison darts. In Australia, where jellyfish stings are common, lifeguard stations keep bottles of vinegar with their safety equipment.

Which one was it, again?

Vinegar MAYO Chili Sauce Peanut Butter

13

Looking for a snack that bites back?

FROM OCTOBER TO MAY, in some of Japan's most elegant dining rooms, chefs cut a delicacy called *fugu* into petal-thin slices, then sculpt them into elaborate flower and bird shapes. Some of the wealthy diners swear the food tastes like chicken. Others say it melts on their tongues. Still others—about 50 every year—fall from their chairs and die.

Fugu is the Japanese name for puffer fish, or blowfish, one of the world's most toxic sea creatures. The poison in its body can cause muscle weakness and paralysis, even in small amounts. But because of the danger involved in consuming the fish, it's become a sought-after item—a dinner table badge of courage.

Foul Fact

Japanese chefs must be specially trained and government licensed to prepare *fugu*.

Garter Snake Surprise

How much have you learned about venom? Test your knowledge by figuring out how 11-year-old Garth was poisoned.

The Clues:

1. Garth's elementary school was in Camarillo, California, where venomous snakes are rare.
2. Garth was playing with a small garter snake. Then the snake whipped its head around and clamped its jaws on Garth's arm, so tightly he couldn't shake it loose.
3. Eventually, the school custodian managed to pry open the snake's jaw with a screwdriver.
4. Everyone was sure it was just a garter snake. But Garth's arm turned an angry red, and then black, and quickly swelled.
5. He was rushed to the hospital, where he lay in serious condition.

What happened?

Answer:

Garth was bitten in 1975, before scientists knew that many snakes and reptiles generally considered harmless do have poisons in their saliva. Garter snakes don't have the kind of fangs that allow them to inject their venom easily, but they do have rear teeth, and Garth's snake bit hard enough and held on for long enough that some of its saliva seeped into the wound, poisoning the boy's arm. After a few days in the hospital, Garth recovered.

EEK!

Chapter 2

BUGGED OUT

We use the word "bug" to refer to a vast variety of skittering, creeping, and crawling creatures—including poisonous ones. Some of them, such as ants and bees, we see every summer. Others, such as the brown recluse spider, are so shy we never notice them. Which is fortunate, because we wouldn't want to feel their toxic effects...

Which spider has scare-power?

IF YOU WANT TO CAST A SPOOKY SPIDER in your next horror film, don't look for it in North America. On the whole continent, there are only two spiders with venom strong enough to kill a human: the brown recluse and the black widow. The brown recluse got its name because it would much rather hide than hunt humans. And the black widow spider hasn't killed anyone in more than 10 years.

For true hair-raising effect, you'll have to try these candidates:

- The funnel-web spider: This Australian arachnid with a cone-shaped web has big fangs and is very aggressive. It killed more than 25 people in the last century (although none since 1981, when an antivenin was developed).

- The Brazilian wandering spider: Also called the banana spider, this nocturnal South American species is the most venomous in the world. It occasionally hitches a ride to Europe or North America in a banana shipment, causing supermarket chaos when it arrives.

- The goliath bird-eating spider: This resident of Central and South America has the leg-span of a dinner plate. Its bite probably wouldn't kill a human... just cause a day or two of excruciating pain.

KING OF THE CREEPY CRAWLIES

South America's giant centipede is as long as a ruler—big enough to hunt small lizards, frogs, and birds. Researchers have even found groups of them hanging upside down in caves, feeding on bats. These creatures can inject venom from their front claws and secrete poison from their legs. They're not quite toxic enough to kill humans, but victims say that getting bitten feels like being skewered with a hot fireplace poker.

Did you hear footsteps?

18

What has eight legs and a tail?

ALTHOUGH WE DON'T THINK OF THEM as bugs, scorpions are actually related to spiders. They stalk their prey at night, grabbing insects, small lizards, and other scorpions with their strong claws. Then they arc their stingers over their backs to inject a complex venom—one that scientists are still working to understand. The way it affects human cells might eventually lead to the development of new painkillers.

Not all scorpions are poisonous, and even the most toxic ones don't usually kill people. You wouldn't want to test them, though. A serious sting can cause a burning sensation, numbness, nausea, and eventually (though rarely) respiratory failure and death.

If you ever see a real scorpion, walk cautiously away. And be glad you didn't meet its ancient ancestor instead. About 400 million years ago, scorpions were the size of large dogs.

All scorpions
must be leashed

19

ARRGH! I think
I preferred boiling oil!

☠ QUESTION 10

Do you hear buzzing?

NOW IN THEATRES: ATTACK OF THE KILLER BEES!

In this B-movie thriller, a scientist crossbreeds gentle North American bees with African pollinators, and creates a deadly super-bug! The creature is spreading steadily north, and may be coming soon to a city near you...

Although it sounds like the plot of a horror film, it's a true story. In 1956, a scientist named Warwick Kerr was working at a university in Brazil, trying to breed a new kind of honeybee. He wanted a creature that could live in Brazil's tropical climate, so he imported a species from Africa. He wanted bees that would mind their own business while sweetly pollinating crops, so he bred the African species with the calm European honeybee. He created... killer bees!

Of course, it's the newspapers that call them killer bees instead of their more formal name, Africanized bees. By either name, they're more dangerous than the common North American species. Their venom is the same as that of regular bees, but they defend their nests with extreme aggression, sending out large and angry swarms at the first sign of trouble. And ever since a substitute beekeeper let them escape from Kerr's laboratory, they've been moving farther north every year. They can now be found across the southern United States, and as far north as Utah.

More than a thousand people have died from killer bee stings since the species was created. Still, unless you kick a nest, your chances of being attacked are extremely low. Scientists say that the best way to react to an attack is to cover your head and run. Then, get inside a car or a house, fast! And don't forget to shut the door behind you.

whoops!

Foul Fact

Bee venom is just as strong as snake venom. Luckily for us, a bee can carry a lot less than a cobra can. Unless you have an allergy, it will take a lot of bee stings to kill you.

When is a bug like an airborne missile?

SPIDERS AND BEES AREN'T THE ONLY BUGS with bite. All sorts of insects have developed unique ways to hunt and protect themselves. There's one creepy creature known as the assassin bug, with a range that extends from South America to Canada to Europe. Using a large, curved tube called a rostrum—like a cross between a nose and a stinger— the bug injects its victims with a paralyzing poison. It can then suck out a blood sample—or the insides of an entire cockroach or caterpillar. When threatened, assassin bugs can shoot or spit their poison, hurling it the length of a human forearm. Scientists have proven they can aim, and some people claim the bugs shoot for the eyes.

The African bombardier beetle is another bug with amazing aim. It has two "tanks" in its belly. One tank holds a chemical called hydroquinone and the other holds hydrogen peroxide. If the beetle is threatened, it blasts the chemicals out of gunlike barrels, and the substances meet and explode in a large bang of poisonous combustion. One beetle can release more than 20 blasts in under a second.

Foul Fact

A bombardier beetle's showy black and yellow stripes send a warning message to predators: "Remember me? I'm too poisonous to eat!" Predators learn quickly that trying to chew on one of these guys is a bad idea, and they avoid them in future. In scientific terms, that's called aposematic coloration. *Apo* means "away" and *sematic* means "sign."

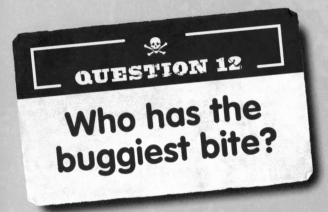

QUESTION 12

Who has the buggiest bite?

DO YOU THINK THE ANTS in your backyard are harmless? That's because you're big and they're small. If you were the size of a beetle, or even a rat, you'd know those ants are dangerous. In fact, common harvester ants are some of the most venomous bugs on the planet—for their size. They can bite with their mandibles, sting with their tails, and chemically signal their friends to come and sting, too.

Harvester ants are fearless in battle. When faced with an intruder or threatened by a neighboring ant colony, they are quick to attack. Researchers tracked one "war" between ant colonies that lasted 46 days.

Only the horned lizard knows how to deal with hundreds of harvester ants. This lizard has a super-fast tongue to snap up the insects before they bite. It swallows them whole, then relies on a thick coating of mucous in its throat and stomach to protect it from stings until the creatures are digested. Yum!

Thank goodness I have a cold.

The Eight-Legged Question

Are you an arachnid expert yet? In May 2009, students in a Manitoba science class were keeping a spider in a jar. What should they have done with it—let it loose in the schoolyard or turned it over to the local conservation officer?

The Clues:

1. The spider was given to the science teacher by a grocery store employee.
2. It had a hairy body, striped legs, and visible fangs.
3. It was about the size of a softball.
4. If bothered, the spider would lift its front legs and wave them aggressively.
5. The spider had arrived at the grocery store with a shipment of bananas.

Answer: Manitoba Conservation quickly confiscated the deadly Brazilian wandering spider, also known as a banana spider for its habit of hiding in bunches of fruit.

Chapter 3

LETHAL LEAVES

An innocent blue flower, a shady tree on a hot tropical day, a tasty-looking bean—these are killers in disguise. Around the world, poisonous plants lurk, some deep in the jungle and some in our own backyards. Nibbling on aconite root has sent hikers to the hospital, and snacking on nightshade berries has sent people to their graves.

Would you recognize a poisonous plant before it bit you back?

A PLANT'S POISONS CAN LURK ANYWHERE—in seeds, in tempting and colorful berries and beans, or in the underground root.

- The seeds of the castor bean plant produce one of the world's most deadly poisons, called ricin. It causes stomach cramps, bleeding, rapid heart rate, and failure of the nervous system. In powdered form, a single bean can be fatal. In 1962, the United States Army actually patented the seeds, hoping to turn them into a potent chemical weapon.

- The deadly nightshade plant tempts people with its plump black berries. Every year, victims are rushed to emergency rooms with nightshade poisoning. The chemicals in the berry cause speeding heart rates, hallucinations, and seizures. In the late 1600s, American colonists in Virginia poisoned British soldiers with a relative of nightshade called jimsonweed. Then they watched happily while the poisoned and hallucinating soldiers battled with feathers, pretended to be monkeys, or fell in love with their friends.

- Another nightshade relative, and one of the world's most ancient poisons, is the mandrake root. Sometimes growing as long as a human leg, and gnarled and twisted like a mutant carrot, the mandrake root might look like a human figure. And it was believed in bygone days that the plant would scream when pulled from the ground—a mysterious scream that would kill anyone near enough to hear it. To avoid death by screaming mandrake root, European harvesters apparently tied their dogs to mandrake plants, then stood far away while the animals pulled the roots from the ground. In low doses, mandrake is a sedative. In higher doses, it quickly kills.

She doesn't look berry well.

27

QUESTION 14

Can leafy greens win a war?

IN ABOUT 600 BC, the city-state of Delphi in ancient Greece went to war with the city-state of Kirrha. A man named Cleisthenes led the attack, sending his navy to block Kirrha's port and his army to surround the walls. Then, he diverted the city's water source, leaving the citizens with nothing to drink for days.

Apparently, Cleisthenes knew the power of a bad case of diarrhea. Just when the people of Kirrha were writhing with thirst, he returned the water flow—after contaminating the spring with leaves from the poisonous hellebore plant.

Talk about a bad case of the runs! Kirrha's soldiers were so thirsty and drank so deeply of the foul water that they were overcome by stomach cramps. When Delphi's army came pounding to the gates, the defenders were all on their toilets. The city was quickly conquered.

FLOWER POWER

In the Harry Potter series, when Professor Snape makes a potion to help werewolf Remus Lupin, he uses a real plant—aconite, also known as wolfsbane. Like many other poisonous plants of the world, aconite looks completely innocent. But hikers have died after eating its roots and gardeners have had racing hearts simply from handling the flowers. Presumably, werewolves have a very different immune system.

How deadly is a death cap?

IT'S CALLED A "DEATH CAP" MUSHROOM for a reason. This little fungus causes 90 percent of the world's mushroom-related deaths. The problem is that it looks like other, safer mushrooms. Even with a field guide to friendly mushrooms, you might have trouble telling it apart from an edible version. And if you stir-fry it with your favorite vegetables, it will taste like the mushrooms you buy at the grocery store.

Then, maybe 8 hours later, maybe 12… a stomachache, diarrhea, vomiting. It gets worse. You can't get enough to drink. Your liver starts to fail, then your kidneys. Without quick hospital treatment—and sometimes even *with* treatment—your kidneys stop working and your body shuts down. Half of one mushroom is enough to kill an adult.

Can trees have fangs?

THE MANCHINEEL TREE SWAYS NEAR THE WATER'S EDGE in Florida, South America, and the Caribbean, its roots protecting the soil from erosion and its branches sheltering visitors from the ocean breezes. Small, green, apple-like fruits dangle, the white sand spreads below, and the shade looks just right for an afternoon nap...

If you don't mind waking up with festering blisters, that is. The manchineel tree is a tower of toxin. Its sap, its leaves, and its fruit harbor seven distinct poisons, each less lovely than the last.

There are a few other highly toxic trees in the world. One of the most infamous is India's tall nux vomica tree, the source of strychnine. Made from crushed seeds, this concoction has been used as a rat poison—and as a murder weapon. It causes such terrible convulsions that victims are unable to breathe. In ancient Malaysia, people used it to execute prisoners.

Africa has its own poisonous trees, which produce a chemical called ratbane. In the early 1900s, colonists in Africa used it to keep rats out of stored food. More recently, it's been used in New Zealand and the United States on animal collars. Ranchers place these collars on sheep and cows, so that a wolf or coyote lunging for its victim's neck gets a mouthful of poison instead.

31

THE FIRST TOXICOLOGISTS

The use of poison to kill pests is just one example of local ingenuity. Around the world, people have found unique uses for the poisonous plants in their own backyards.

- Kenyan cave paintings from 18,000 years ago show weapons with small hollows in them. Researchers believe the Masai people used these dips to hold deadly plant extracts—the first known use of poisoned weapons.

- Centuries ago, traditional European healers used small amounts of poisonous hemlock to calm or sedate their patients.

- In South and Central America, people used the ground bark of the Jamaica dogwood tree to stun fish and make them easier to net.

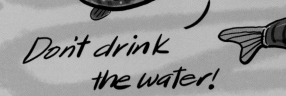

Don't drink the water!

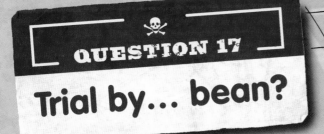

Trial by... bean?

Guilty!

IN THE 1840S, EUROPEAN MISSIONARIES working in Nigeria heard rumors of secret trials. Apparently, people accused of witchcraft were forced to eat a certain bean, called esere. According to this test, those who died must have been guilty. Those who survived were most certainly innocent. And the in-between—the people who became sick but avoided death—were sold into slavery because they couldn't be trusted.

The Christian missionaries thought all of this was highly offensive to God. The practice would have to be stopped, at once. And if these poisonous esere beans could be found and sent to England for further study, that would be good, too.

There was only one problem: no one could find esere.

Finally, in 1855, a missionary named Reverend Waddell discovered that a local king held a bean monopoly. The king had ordered all esere plants destroyed, except for those in his royal garden. That way, he controlled the witchcraft trials. Reverend Waddell managed to obtain some of the seeds and smuggle them to England. In 1859, another missionary sent home a sprig of a live plant.

Back in Europe, toxicologist Robert Christison tested the new arrivals by the best method available at the time—he swallowed a tiny piece of a seed. He noticed that his heart slowed down immediately. Eventually, scientists discovered a toxic chemical in the esere bean. Its strength depends partly on the ripeness of the plant and partly on whether the bean is chewed or swallowed whole, which helps explain why some people lived while others died. Unless, of course, the dead really were witches.

MEAN BEANS

Can a regular jar of green beans be poisonous? Only if you're sharing your food with the bacteria that produces botulin toxin, one of the world's most powerful poisons. It affects the nervous system, gradually causing paralysis in the face and arms, and eventually shutting down the lungs.

Most cases of botulism are caused by badly preserved food, which is why people check to make sure their jars are properly sealed (the jar should make a *pop* or *whoosh* sound when it's opened). Major botulism outbreaks are rare. Today, it's more common to hear of botulism as the main ingredient in the cosmetic treatment Botox. Used in tiny amounts, it can weaken small facial muscles and make wrinkles less noticeable.

Botulism
Beans

Good
'N'
Deadly

Botulism
Beans

Botulism
Beans

B

Good
'N'

Good
'N'

Good
'N'

Down on the Docks

At the Liverpool harbor in 1864, workers were busily unloading a merchant ship. Until something strange happened. The children who usually scampered about the docks, causing mischief and getting in the way, were clutching their stomachs.

Can you use your leaf lore to figure out why?

The Clues:

1. The ship had come from West Africa.
2. The children appeared to be snacking on dried beans—some had eaten half a bean, others had swallowed up to six.
3. Almost 60 children were soon vomiting, shaking, dizzy, and, in some cases, unable to walk.
4. At the local hospital, they were given sulfate of zinc and mustard water to purge their systems.
5. One boy died. The others eventually recovered.

Answer:

On board the merchant ship was a container of esere, smuggled out of Africa. When the seeds spilled on the dock, the hungry children snatched them up and ate them—with disastrous results. A similar accident happened seven years later. By that time, doctors had figured out that atrophine—the poison produced by nightshade—neutralized the toxin of esere and acted as a cure. They used one poison to counteract the other.

Chapter 4

MURDEROUS MINERALS

Almost 2000 years ago, a Greek chemist named Agathodian placed a piece of copper into a solution of arsenic trioxide and watched it turn a brilliant green. Scientists now know that Agathodian created a poisonous compound called copper arsenite, something that would cause all sorts of problems when it was "rediscovered" hundreds of years later.

Of course, copper arsenite isn't the only mineral with dangerous properties. In different places in the world, people are drinking water laced with arsenic. Or eating mercury-battered fish and chips. When people and minerals meet accidentally, or when scientists create new chemical combinations, terrible things can happen.

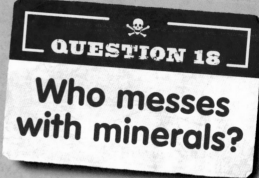

Who messes with minerals?

DEEP IN AN UNDERGROUND LABORATORY, an alchemist cackles over his latest concoction. Striving to create precious gold from base minerals such as lead, or to discover the secret to long life, maybe even immortality, he sits surrounded by bubbling potions. If only he could find the elusive philosopher's stone, long believed to hold the key to unlock the mysteries of his art!

It may seem like something from science fiction, but alchemy was a serious pursuit in the 1600s and 1700s, and a few alchemists still practice today. Alchemists were not mad scientists, either. Although they worked in secret to protect their discoveries, some were highly respected members of European society. Sir Isaac Newton, the man who explained gravity, was also a dedicated alchemist. And King Charles II, ruler of England in the mid-1600s, had his own laboratory in the palace basement. If he succeeded in turning rock into gold, imagine how rich his country would become!

Unfortunately, Charles used mercury in his experiments, and he may have accidentally killed himself. He died on February 6, 1685, after suffering from convulsions, muscle paralysis, and breathing difficulties—all possible symptoms of mercury poisoning.

At last, the secret to long life!

Why was the mad hatter mad?

It's my best creation yet!

THERE'S AN OLD-FASHIONED EXPRESSION that describes someone who seems a bit nutty as being "mad as a hatter"—like the Mad Hatter in *Alice's Adventures in Wonderland*. Why would a hatter be especially "mad"? It has to do with mercury poisoning.

To get rabbit or beaver fur to matt into felt, hat-makers would partially dissolve the hairs with a chemical called mercury nitrate. Then, as the hatters cut and shaped the felt, they breathed in the mercury dust. Researchers now believe that almost half of all 19th-century hatters suffered from chronic mercury poisoning—they were irritable, illogical, and paranoid. They talked constantly, and not always reasonably. In essence, they were "mad as hatters." And hatters weren't the only ones.

For centuries, people have used mercury for all sorts of industrial purposes. It has made its way into the environment from the burning of fossil fuels and the disposal of medical and municipal waste. For humans and animals, exposure is dangerous. One of the problems with mercury is that it builds up in the body. Mercury released into the water, for example—often because of industrial waste—can be absorbed by algae and eaten by small fish. When big fish eat many small fish, they absorb all the accumulated mercury. Then the big fish swim off to the local sushi restaurant or the tuna fish cannery.

The good news? The world is working to decrease the amount of mercury that makes its way into our environment. A scientist named William Shotyk has studied peat bogs in Greenland and the Faroe Islands to measure the amount of mercury trapped in the ground. What he found was that, 14,000 years ago, there was very little mercury in the ground, but as civilization grew more industrial, the amount greatly increased. Mercury exposure peaked in the 1950s, with levels 100 times higher than the earliest measurements. And today, now that we know the dangers of mercury to people and the environment, efforts to reduce mercury exposure have brought that number down again by 90 percent.

DOCTORED TO DEATH

In December 1799, retired American president George Washington complained of a fever and a sore throat. His doctors sprang into action. They extracted blood—many people believed that patients suffered from having too much blood, infected or weakened blood, or blood that was not properly circulating. Doctors thought patients could be helped if some of the blood was removed. They dosed him with calomel, a mercury-based "medicine." They bled him again, and dosed him again.

When he failed to improve, they gave him another poisonous mixture, called tartar emetic, to help him sweat out the sickness. Then, hoping to suck out the infection, they slathered his throat with a blistering compound made of crushed beetles. They prepared a poultice of vinegar. And finally, they blistered the soles of his feet, believing that it would draw the fever down from his head.

George Washington died one day after his illness began.

This will make him feel better.

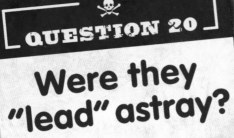
Were they "lead" astray?

That meal was a bit heavy.

IN 1845, A BRITISH EXPLORER NAMED SIR JOHN FRANKLIN set sail for the Arctic. He was searching for the Northwest Passage, a fabled waterway through the ice that would link the Atlantic and Pacific oceans. Along with two ships and 129 men, he carried 8000 tins of food, and high-tech systems to turn seawater into drinking water.

Franklin's entire expedition disappeared.

Between 1847 and 1880, 26 expeditions went in search of the missing explorers. They found a few clues—three graves, some Inuit witnesses, and a letter. Finally, in 1981, more than a century after Franklin disappeared, a University of Alberta anthropologist named Owen Beattie found more remains and suggested some answers.

It seems that the men died of pneumonia, tuberculosis, and starvation. For men with fresh water and plentiful food, they had grown surprisingly weak. The answer lay in the men's hair. When it was analyzed, it was found to contain high levels of lead. This could have seeped into the food from the solder that welded the tins closed. Or it could have seeped into the water from the distilling system. Whatever the source, Franklin's men discovered first-hand the symptoms of lead poisoning: abdominal pain, digestive problems, weight loss, nervous system disruption, coma, and death.

SUGARY DREAMS

Would you care for a teaspoon of lead in your tea? In 1850, British sugar refineries wanted to treat crushed sugarcane with lead to help purify it. They argued they would be using minute amounts of the mineral—hardly enough to poison anyone. Thankfully, officials decided not to approve the process.

One poison or two, sir?

Can you paint yourself to death?

FOR CENTURIES, PAINTERS HAVE USED MINERAL-BASED PAINTS. Cadmium makes yellows, oranges, and reds; lead oxide, a pure white; and cinnabar (a type of mercury), a vibrant vermilion red. All of these minerals can be dangerous even in small amounts, and lead is infamous for giving artists an ailment known as "painter's colic."

Sometimes, exposure has been fatal. In 1952, the Brazilian government asked artist Candido Portinari to create two murals for the United Nations. Candido worked for years on the panels—one of war and one of peace—

but in the middle of the project was so ill that doctors recommended he stop painting altogether. Ignoring their advice, Candido completed the work in 1956 and continued making smaller pieces until he died of lead poisoning in 1962.

Painters weren't the only ones suffering. In the 1950s, there was lead in gasoline, in house paint, and even in some foods. The paint in your grandparents' home might have been up to half lead! Children today are exposed to much less of this mineral—unless, of course, they play with tainted toys.

In 2007, millions of toys were recalled after hazardous lead levels were found in the paint. Fortunately, the toy companies discovered the problem and replaced the toys before any children were harmed.

A glass of water, anyone?

OOPS... THIS WATER IS MIXED WITH A LITTLE HUMAN WASTE. And maybe a touch of industrial runoff from factories and mills upstream.

In the 1980s, that's all the people in Bangladesh had to drink. The rivers and ponds were so polluted that children were getting terribly ill—often with diphtheria, an illness caused by bacteria. Some were even dying. To solve the problem, international agencies paid for tube wells. These miniature wells—about the diameter of a baseball— were drilled through the earth to tap water sources about 30 metres (100 feet) below the surface. And they worked! They were so successful that soon every village had its own version. No more diarrhea.

For a while, everything went well. Then, slowly, skin diseases began to appear. There were more problems during pregnancies. Cancer rates rose. But because disease in Bangladesh wasn't tracked the same way it would have been in an industrialized country, it was *years* before people from the international agencies noticed the trend.

When investigators finally discovered the culprit—it was arsenic. The mineral had been lying deep in the soil, seeping into the water that flows naturally beneath the ground. It had always been there, but until the tube wells reached down to it, it had never been a problem. Arsenic poisoning can cause all your body's organs to fail, and is believed to be a cause of many types of cancer. By the time health officials figured this out, there were 10 million tube wells in the country. Millions had been poisoned. And the people of Bangladesh were once again facing their original problem—there was no safe water.

Today, researchers are still scratching their heads for a solution. Some suggest new, deeper wells. Others recommend water purifiers. But they all agree on three things: there are too many people; there are too few clean water sources; and there's not enough money in Bangladesh to solve the problem.

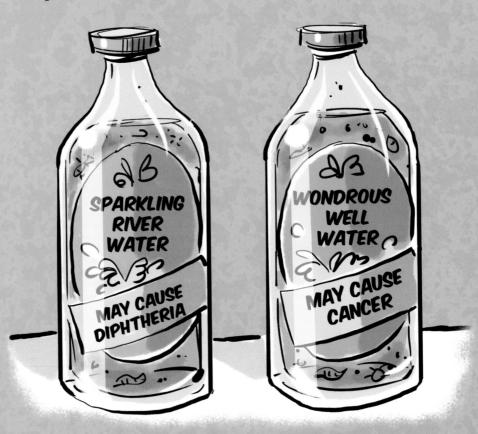

We promise to stop poisoning the Earth...soon... sometime...later... ...eventually.

QUESTION 23

Who will win the bromide brawl?

A FIGHT OVER FARMING PRACTICES has been brewing for years in the United States. On one side of the arena: labor unions, environmentalists, scientists, and public health organizations. On the other side: agricultural companies and the chemical corporations nicknamed the "Bromide Barons."

Some companies say that they can't make a profit raising strawberries, tomatoes, and flowers without using methyl bromide to sterilize the soil. Treating the dirt with this chemical gets rid of any insect pests that might munch on young seedlings. So far, no one's found an alternative that's equally cheap and effective.

The other side argues that when this pesticide drifts over fields it's dangerous to people who live and work in agricultural areas. They say the chemical causes headaches, blurry vision, and even lung, kidney, and nervous system damage. Plus, methyl bromide depletes the ozone layer, and the United States has signed an international agreement promising to stop spreading the poison. Some environmentalists fear that if the United States uses methyl bromide, developing countries will follow that example.

So far, neither side has achieved victory. The U.S. claims that fumigating the agricultural fields is a "critical use" of the chemical, and so shouldn't be restricted by the international agreement.

The fight continues...

PESKY PESTICIDES

From the 1920s to the 1960s, methyl mercury was used by seed companies as a disinfectant and a fungicide. Dousing seeds in the chemical kept them fresh and free of the fungi that can damage crops and make it hard for farmers to earn a living. And everyone assumed that once the seeds were planted in soil, the possibly poisonous chemical residue would wash away harmlessly. There was just one problem—sometimes, the seeds weren't planted.

In the early 1970s, a huge shipment of seeds was on its way to Iraq. Because of the long voyage ahead, the seeds were treated with fungicide so that they would not be moldy when they arrived. But the shipment arrived just after the planting season ended, so farmers looked for other uses for the seeds. When the seeds were fed to livestock or ground into flour and sold to families, at least 450 people died.

The Mercury's Rising

In the 1960s, Hydro-Québec built a series of new dams in central Canada and flooded large wilderness valleys. Soon after, native groups in the area fell ill, and doctors discovered mercury poisoning. Where did the mercury come from?

The Clues:
1. The affected native groups ate diets high in local fish.
2. Dam-builders guaranteed the dams were 100% mercury-free.
3. Local industries proclaimed their innocence. They only dumped their waste downstream.
4. There were no signs of sabotage.
5. Hydro-Québec solved the problem by emptying the new reservoirs and then refilling them.

What happened?

Answer:

The solution lay in the soil. Mercury naturally collects in soil, which is what happened in the forests of Quebec. When the land was suddenly flooded, that mercury dissolved into the water. It poisoned the fish, which poisoned the people. When Hydro-Québec emptied and refilled the reservoirs, it was like flushing a giant bowl of mercury-contaminated toilet water. The new water was relatively poison-free.

Ah! Fresh air!

Chapter 5

GAS BLASTS

Poisonous gases can erupt from volcanic craters or explode on the battlefield. They can spew from chimneys or seep from rusty canisters deep in the ocean. Carbon monoxide, chlorine, and sarin—these foul fumes have one thing in common. They're gases that humans were never meant to breathe.

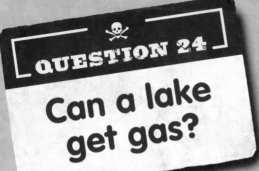

Can a lake get gas?

NESTLED IN A FERTILE CAMEROON VALLEY, Lake Nyos is a still, deep blue. It looks as picturesque and perfect as any other large lake—but this one holds a secret. Formed in a volcanic crater, the lake is constantly fed carbon dioxide from cracks far beneath the surface.

Usually, this gas dissolves into the water and mud at the lake bottom and stays there, held down by the pressure of the deep waters above. But late in the evening of August 21, 1986, something changed. The gas erupted from the depths, sending a bubble, then another, then a geyser shooting from the waters.

Carbon dioxide is always present in our environment—we expel it when we breathe. It makes up about 0.036 percent of the air around us. Most of the time it's perfectly harmless and we aren't aware of it at all. But if we sit in a crowded classroom with all the doors and windows closed, the carbon dioxide level might climb to 1 percent, and make us sleepy. It's only when it climbs to more than 4 percent that it becomes poisonous—toxic enough to kill.

At Lake Nyos that night, a cloud of carbon dioxide formed and rolled down the nearby mountain slopes, killing birds and cattle along the way. When it reached the homes of farmers and townspeople, it invaded like an invisible storm. The next day, a few hardy survivors woke from coma-like sleeps to find 1700 people dead.

The people who lived near Lake Nyos were exposed to carbon dioxide levels far higher than 4 percent, and only a few survived. Today, pipes collect the water at the bottom of that lake and feed it slowly to the surface, ensuring that another deadly collection of gas will never bubble from the bottom.

I don't think that's Old Faithful.

QUESTION 25

What's worse than a sunburn?

THE WEATHER FORECAST for the Big Island of Hawaii this week: voggy with a chance of laze.

We think of Hawaii as the land of beaches and surfboards, ukuleles and grass skirts. But there are also massive, active, poison-belching volcanoes there. When these volcanoes erupt, they spew forth gases. In fact, scientists say that except for oxygen (which is produced by plants), all the gases in our atmosphere come from under the earth, via volcanic activity. So when the Kilauea Volcano on the Big Island of Hawaii begins to rumble, there are two dangers.

The first is called "vog," or volcanic smog. That's what happens when a crater releases sulfur dioxide, and the gas reacts with the air to form sulfate aerosols—tiny chemical particles suspended in the air—and dangerous sulfuric acid. The drops of these toxins hang around like fog, circling the island's peaks with poisonous gas. Vog is thought to cause health hazards including lung damage, headaches, sore throats, and breathing difficulties.

The second danger is laze. A mix of hydrochloric acid and seawater, laze shoots into the air when bubbling lava hits the ocean. These plumes can shower down a foul form of rainwater that stings like lemon juice. It can also contaminate the rainwater supplies used by residents.

Sometimes, due to excessive vog or laze, people are warned to stay inside. Schoolchildren spend their lunch hours indoors and people with chronic conditions such as asthma keep their medications nearby.

The mountains of Hawaii aren't the only ones that send noxious fumes into the atmosphere. Other active volcanoes rumble around the world. And some volcanoes that haven't erupted for hundreds of years can still emit gas—enough to kill large swaths of trees, and keep people and wildlife away.

Foul Fact

There's an upside to volcanic gases. Scientists can measure them to help predict when future eruptions might occur.

Why do you smoke that garbage?

What are those garbage dumps smoking?

HAVE YOU EVER SMELLED BURNING PLASTIC? Or seen black smoke billow from smoldering car tires? When we burn waste, we release all the poisons inside and send them spiraling into the atmosphere.

Some of the worst gases from the garbage heap are:

• carbon dioxide, which contributes to global warming

• sulfur dioxide, which causes acid rain

• oxides of nitrogen, which help create smog

It gets worse! Old electronic products give off mercury, lead, and cadmium. Styrofoam takeout containers turn into styrene vapors and dioxins, both cancer-causing chemicals. And plastics turn into dioxins and furans—more poison.

If reading about this is making it hard to breathe, don't panic. In North America, recycling programs and high-tech incinerators are helping with the problem. Researchers have even found ways to turn incinerator gases into energy sources.

But incinerators aren't always properly built or regulated, especially in newly industrialized countries. China has been criticized for incinerators that fill cities with choking smoke. And according to environmentalists, incinerators everywhere would be a lot less nasty and a lot more helpful if there wasn't so much garbage in the first place.

What's a gas attack?

IMAGINE YOU'RE A SOLDIER in World War I. It's April 22, 1915, and you've been living in a cold, wet trench in the Ypres battlefield for weeks, trying to defend Belgium from the Germans. Your entire world has been reduced to a stalemate of mud-covered men shooting at each other across mud-covered fields.

But on this evening, dusk brings something different. First, a jaw-rattling bombardment from the Germans' big field guns. Then, a silent, olive-colored mist rolling toward you and sinking into the trenches. And then panic.

When the Germans opened 5700 chlorine gas canisters that morning and let the wind carry the poison over the field, they killed more than 5000 Allied soldiers in 10 minutes. Men dropped to the ground, unable to breathe, while others tried to scramble backward through the mud. Two thousand survivors were captured.

The Germans also used another type of gas, mustard gas, in the Third Battle of Ypres, in 1917. Mustard gas caused skin blisters, terrible bleeding, choking, and blindness.

By the end of the war, 400,000 soldiers had died from exposure to these new weapons, and millions more were injured. Because the gas causes lung damage, even victims who survived the attacks spent many weeks in the hospital. That meant thousands of soldiers were in treatment instead of on the battlefield—something that weakened the Allied numbers and, in terms of war, made mustard gas a highly effective weapon.

Chemical weapons were banned worldwide by the Geneva Convention in 1925. But that didn't stop countries from mass-producing and stockpiling mustard gas. And once it was made and ready, it proved too tempting to resist. Britain, France, Italy, Japan, Poland, Russia, Egypt, and Iraq were all accused of using mustard gas *after* the Geneva Convention.

Foul Fact

Mustard gas has nothing to do with mustard, the yellow goop we put on hot dogs. It just happens to smell the same.

DOWN IN THE DUMPS

After World War II, German stockpiles of mustard gas were dumped into the Baltic Sea… proving that what goes down must eventually come up again. For more than 40 years, fishing boats have been accidentally hooking chemicals from the sea, sometimes with hazardous results—the barrels are as dangerous now as they were when they sank.

In 2008, a group of American scientists tried to track thousands of tons of chemical weapons dumped into the oceans by the U.S. and other countries between 1942 and 1972. They used coordinates and maps to pinpoint dump sites, tracked currents, and pored through old government records to determine where the barrels might be. Here's the answer they came up with:

We have no idea.

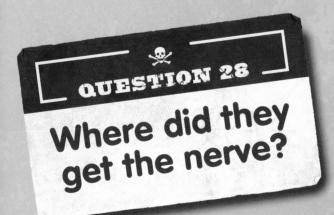
Where did they get the nerve?

IN THE EARLY 1900s, when European chemists were messing around with chlorine and mustard gas and a boatload of other noxious chemicals, they came up with a particularly nasty set called nerve agents.

We all know that our nerves tell our muscles when to move. They're also in charge of telling muscles when to *stop* moving. They do that with a special enzyme. Unless, of course, they've been hit with a nerve agent. Then the enzyme doesn't work, and the nerves can't say stop.

One of the most infamous nerve agents is sarin, developed by Nazi scientists during World War II. It's invisible, tasteless, and odorless... and 500 times more toxic than cyanide. Victims lose consciousness and suffer convulsions, paralysis, and respiratory failure. Even a tiny amount of sarin in the air or on the skin can cause such symptoms as confusion, nausea, and weakness.

During the Cold War, from the 1940s to 1980s, the United States and Russia both stockpiled sarin, ready to use in case World War III broke out. Sarin was also produced and used by Iraq under Saddam Hussein. It was one of many chemical weapons banned by the United Nations in 1993.

I believe we have the advantage.

TOXIC TRAIN

Aum Shinrikyo was a Japanese religious cult with up to 40,000 worldwide members and a few key businesses—including a laboratory that could produce anthrax, the Ebola virus, and other biological nightmares.

Apparently, no one thought to be concerned about a cult with a chemical weapons factory. Until 1994. That's when members drove a truck onto a street in the city of Matsumoto and released a cloud of toxic sarin gas. Two hundred people went to the hospital and seven died.

Then, in 1995, five cult members carried bags of sarin onto a Tokyo subway train. As the train pulled into a station, they used sharpened umbrella tips to puncture the bags and hopped off the train, leaving a trail of gasping travelers in their wake. Twelve people died and thousands suffered poisoning symptoms.

After the subway attack, police raided the cult's properties and arrested 200 people.

Shaky Shelter

The wind screamed and the ice crackled on March 11, 1990, as forest ranger Fred Richter struggled to find shelter. He was patrolling California's Mammoth Mountain, a volcanic peak caught in the thick of a winter blizzard. Finally, through the swirling snow, Fred spotted the roof of an old cabin poking through the drifts. He lowered himself down to safety—and almost died.

The Clues:

1. Fred's heart pounded and his legs buckled under him. He was gasping for air.
2. On the verge of losing consciousness, Fred pulled himself up through the roof and into the blizzard. There he slowly recovered.
3. Only the tip of the cabin's roof was visible beside him. The rest of the building was buried in the snow.

What happened?

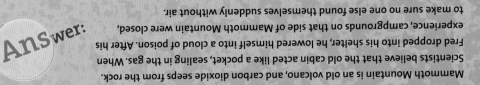

Answer: Mammoth Mountain is an old volcano, and carbon dioxide seeps from the rock. Scientists believe that the old cabin acted like a pocket, sealing in the gas. When Fred dropped into his shelter, he lowered himself into a cloud of poison. After his experience, campgrounds on that side of Mammoth Mountain were closed, to make sure no one else found themselves suddenly without air.

You are a real fungi. Here's lunch!

Chapter 6

VILE VILLAINS

If you're an empress, and you're not getting along with your husband, why not slip him a plate of poisoned mushrooms? It worked for Agrippina, the empress of Rome 2000 years ago. Historians say that Agrippina was worried that her husband, Claudius, was going to select a new heir to his throne. She murdered him, ensuring that her son would become the emperor.

Since then, countless murderers have given up their daggers and swords in favor of a few drops of hemlock or a sip of thallium. And we only know about the ones who were caught.

Can a potion cure paranoia?

KING MITHRIDATES OF PONTUS, enemy of the Roman Empire about 2000 years ago, lived in fear that his foes would poison him. The popular poisons of the time came from venomous creatures or from deadly plants such as henbane or hemlock. To protect himself, Mithridates began taking small amounts of each toxin, hoping to build his immunity. He also experimented with a wide range of possible antidotes, until he created what he thought was the perfect, universal cure.

Today, scientists agree that Mithridates's antidotes were mostly useless. But something in his immunity-building regime must have worked. When the Romans finally defeated Pontus, he tried to commit suicide by poisoning himself. He couldn't! The toxic concoction he cooked up managed to kill his wife and his children, but it didn't work on the king.

According to some tales, Mithridates then asked a trusted servant to stab him to death. Other histories say the king was alive to face his enemies, and died by their swords.

AN ADDLED ANTIDOTE

After years of experimentation, Mithridates came up with an antidote that was supposed to work for every poison.

Mithridates's Universal Antidote
Designed (but in no way guaranteed) to counteract the effects of any poison:

1. Squeeze the poisons from 50 plants.
2. Boil a legless lizard.
3. Extract musk from a beaver's scent glands.
4. Mix all of the above.
5. Add honey until tasty.

Mithridates's antidote was used for hundreds of years, but it wasn't a real cure. If people treated with his concoction survived a scorpion bite or a nightshade encounter, they probably would have lived anyway.

You want what?

Roses are red,
violets are blue.
You will be dead
when I poison you.

QUESTION 30

Who gave the death sentence?

EARLY POISON RESEARCH was a dark and dangerous business. And some of the researchers were dark and dangerous, too. Like Nicander of Colophon. He was a doctor who lived in the second century BC and wrote medical books on the subject of venoms and poisons—in the form of poetry! Does that sound crazy? Well, it gets worse. Nicander gained his noxious know-how by poisoning convicted criminals at the local prison. He tested antidotes, too, but they didn't always work.

By the 1500s, scientists had learned much more about poisons. Enough that Catherine de Medici, Queen of France, was able to keep a personal collection of vile potions tucked away in 200 locked cabinets. According to some tales, she would test these poisons while pretending to be on charitable visits to the poor and sick. Then again, many historians say these "experiments" were only rumors, spread by Catherine's enemies.

By the 1800s, the study of poisons—even the research done by murderers—had paid off, and some poisons were used for their positive effects in common medical practice. For example, patients needing surgery in that era might have been dosed with curare. The South American vine extract was first used by hunters—an arrow rubbed in sap would drop animals in their tracks and make birds fall from trees. On the operating table, curare could temporarily paralyze patients, keeping them perfectly still. There was only one problem—they could still feel *everything*.

Just try to catch me!

SITTING PRETTY

In 1867, a researcher named John Harley had an interesting idea. Why not dose hyperactive children with hemlock? A small amount of the poison would paralyze their legs, forcing the children to sit still.

Thankfully, Harley's methods were never used in schools.

More cookies, Mom?

What's the perfect murder weapon?

IT WOULD HAVE TO BE ODORLESS, tasteless, and dissolve easily in liquid. The symptoms should be slow to appear, and they should be mysterious—hard to pin to any specific substance. A stomachache, for example, or joint pain.

Might these people have come close to pulling off the perfect crime?

- In 1953, Mrs. Fletcher poisoned her husband in New South Wales, Australia. For 11 days he endured excruciating joint pain. His hair fell out. Doctors couldn't find the cause... until after his death.

- Graham Young had a wicked stepmother right out of an English fairytale. She smashed his toys and locked him out of the house. In 1962, when Graham was 14 years old, he started slipping poison into her food and drinks, until she wasted away and died.

- In Florida in 1988, a man grew tired of his neighbors' loud parties and barking dogs. He slipped into their kitchen and poured poison into their soda supplies. All were poisoned, and one eventually died.

These killers all used thallium, a poison that causes stomach cramps, then joint pains and insomnia, and finally death. It's not quite the perfect weapon, though. Victims can lose their hair (a telltale sign), and traces of thallium stay in the bones. Mrs. Fletcher was caught when doctors performed an autopsy on her husband. The Florida murderer bragged to an undercover police officer. And Graham Young? He was caught, but only after poisoning several more friends and family members.

BETWEEN JUNE 1980 AND MARCH 1981 —the space of less than a year—36 babies died in Toronto's Hospital for Sick Children.

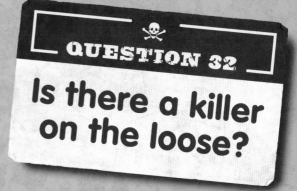

QUESTION 32

Is there a killer on the loose?

It was a place where kids were supposed to be getting better, not dying. As the numbers rose, suspicion fell on a nurse named Susan Nelles. She was arrested and charged with murdering four infants. The public and the media suspected her of killing far more.

Lawyers argued that Susan deliberately overdosed the babies with digoxin, a heart medication derived from the foxglove plant that can save lives in the right dose, but can be deadly in greater amounts. But after a 44-day hearing, a judge decided there wasn't enough evidence to continue the case—and Susan hadn't had access to one of the babies.

So if she didn't kill them, who did?

A royal commission investigated, concluding that 8 deaths were definitely murders and 15 more were suspicious. Accusations fell on other members of the hospital nursing staff, and the stress led several to leave their jobs. One even attempted suicide.

Did someone get away with murder? In the years since, some researchers have suggested the babies weren't murdered after all. They believe that a bad batch of drugs was responsible. Another expert argues that a chemical from rubber intravenous tubing poisoned the children.

Now that so many years have passed, it's unlikely we'll ever know for sure.

NASTY NURSING

In 2003, police arrested a New Jersey nurse named Charles Cullen, accusing him of murdering a patient at the local medical center. A day later, Charles confessed—and said he'd killed up to 40 other patients as well. Some he poisoned with digoxin. Others with insulin overdoses. He's now serving 18 life sentences.

If all your friends took cyanide, would you?

CYANIDE CAN BE FOUND IN APPLE SEEDS and car exhaust, bacteria and burnt plastic. Scientists have even detected it in outer space. Mines douse ore with cyanide to help extract gold and silver. Doctors use it to lower blood pressure. Poachers use it to stun and capture tropical fish.

In mammals, cyanide prevents cells from being able to use oxygen. People lose consciousness quite quickly from even a small dose, and then the heart stops. The chemical hit the headlines in 1978, when it was used in a mass murder-suicide in Jonestown, Guyana. American cult leader Jim Jones had pledged to create a perfect agricultural settlement in Guyana, where everyone worked and everyone benefited from the harvest. Soon, his settlement had almost 1000 residents.

Back in the United States, authorities had concerns about Jonestown. They had heard that no one was allowed to leave, that protesters were punished or drugged, and that Jones himself was taking drugs.

When a congressman decided to visit and investigate the colony, he was shot by the colony's "Red Brigade" guards. Jones declared his colony a failure. That same day, he instructed his followers to commit "revolutionary suicide" by swallowing a cyanide-laced drink or by squirting syringes filled with the poison into their children's mouths. They obeyed, and 918 people died. Investigators believe that Jones shot himself once the poisonings were over.

Foul Fact

Think you're safe from cyanide poisoning because you know that cyanide smells like almonds? Think again. Only 40 to 60 percent of people can detect cyanide's odor.

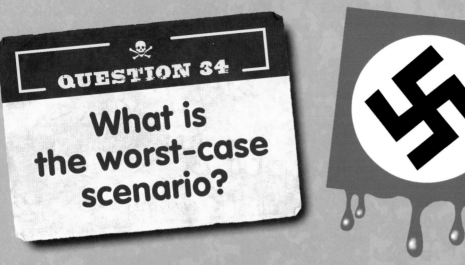

What is the worst-case scenario?

HISTORY'S MOST DEADLY and malicious poisoners worked on a massive scale—through the Nazi death camps of World War II. Under orders from Adolf Hitler, Nazi leaders built a series of gas chambers. They were to exterminate the Jewish people, along with prisoners of war, people with disabilities, Roma people, homosexuals, and others.

The first was in Poland, at Auschwitz. There, soldiers tested an insecticide called Zyklon B on a group of 850 prisoners. They sprinkled pellets through a vent and into a locked chamber full of people, where the insecticide reacted with the air to form a toxic gas. Twenty minutes later, the prisoners were dead and the experiment was deemed a success.

The soldiers built four permanent gas chambers at the camp and proceeded to import prisoners by train, until they were killing 8000 people each day. More than a million people were murdered at Auschwitz before it was liberated by Allied troops in 1945. Over 3 million more were killed at other Polish death camps. In total, at least 11 million people were killed by the Nazis, all across Europe.

Foul Fact

Zyklon B was an insecticide invented by Fritz Haber, the same scientist who created chlorine gas and helped adapt it for use in World War I. But Fritz was Jewish, and left Germany before World War II began. He didn't live to see how Zyklon B was used against Jews.

The Case of the Umbrella Murderer

Georgi Markov was born in 1929 in Bulgaria, where the government controlled the media. As an adult, he fled to Britain. There, he worked for the British Broadcasting Corporation, writing scripts that were highly critical of the Soviet Union. He died suddenly in 1978. Can you figure out how?

The Clues:

1. Georgi was standing at a London bus stop when he felt a jab in his leg. A man holding an umbrella apologized for bumping him, and walked away.
2. When the pain in Georgi's leg wouldn't go away, he told his friends at work. Then he developed a fever and headed for the local hospital.
3. Georgi's heart rate increased, and his stomach cramped... he told doctors that he'd been poisoned. The doctors thought Georgi had the flu.
4. He died three days after being admitted to hospital.
5. In the autopsy, doctors found a small metal pellet in his leg.

Answer:

The umbrella stab was responsible for the pellet in his leg, and the pellet contained ricin, a deadly poison from castor beans. Years later, the "umbrella murder" was pinned on a Bulgarian secret service agent code-named Piccadilly. If the doctors at the London hospital had been familiar with ricin poisoning, they may have taken Georgi's symptoms more seriously. But they wouldn't have been able to save him—work on a ricin vaccine didn't begin until 2004.

Chapter 7

SPILLS & DISASTERS

Dump poison into a river, and the people downstream might get sick. Bury poison underground, and the people who live above it might get sick. It's predictable, right? Well, this chapter is full of stories about poisonous spills and disasters around the world—places where people failed to predict the obvious. They never wondered (or maybe they never cared) what would happen if a safety valve failed or a canister exploded. Often, innocent people paid the price.

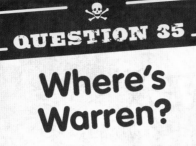
Where's Warren?

BHOPAL, INDIA, IS NICKNAMED THE CITY OF LAKES and known for its natural beauty. But don't drink the water there. And you might want to hold your breath, too.

The Union Carbide chemical plant in Bhopal produced pesticides for use by Indian farmers. But on December 3, 1984, large amounts of water entered a tank full of volatile chemicals. The water and the chemicals reacted to create a hot, poisonous gas, and the tank exploded, releasing a massive cloud of death over the region. Toxic gas drifted through the city air, choking and killing an estimated 8000 people. The death toll continued to climb afterwards.

Union Carbide said the disaster was not their fault. It was sabotage. They claimed that an angry ex-employee dumped the water into the chemical tank and caused the explosion.

Local residents say that safety standards in Bhopal were much lower than those at American Union Carbide plants, and the methods used to make pesticides in Bhopal weren't properly tested. In Bhopal, they say, the equipment was rusty and poorly maintained, and cost-saving shortcuts were used. Employees received inadequate training, and no emergency plans were in place for such a disaster.

Although the Indian government estimated cleanup costs at $3.3 billion, Union Carbide handed over its insurance payment plus interest—$470 million—and settled the government lawsuit.

However, private lawsuits are still ongoing. Every year, Bhopal

Boardroom

KEEP OUT

residents and activists march through the town and burn an effigy of Warren Anderson, the CEO of Union Carbide when the disaster occurred. He's wanted for trial in India. But Warren's over 80 years old and living in the United States. He's not likely to return to India anytime soon. Though he's never been to court, eight local officials were tried in 2010 and convicted of "death by negligence."

THE AFTERMATH

Union Carbide built a hospital in Bhopal, and attempted to settle lawsuits with many survivors. So, if the toxic chemicals that caused the Union Carbide explosion had been cleaned up—if the factory had been dismantled and the contaminated soil carted away—then life in Bhopal might have slowly returned to normal. But no one removed the chemicals.

The government says it's the company's responsibility. But Union Carbide was bought by Dow Chemical in 1999. Since that was 15 years after the disaster, Dow Chemical takes no responsibility for the clean-up. Meanwhile, more babies in the area are being born with physical and mental disabilities—the newest victims of the explosion. And a 1999 Greenpeace study found high levels of mercury in the groundwater—millions of times higher than safe levels.

74

INVEST NOW
LoveCanal
THE IDEAL FAMILY NEIGHBORHOOD
THIS PIPE DREAM BROUGHT TO YOU BY W.T.LOVE

OVER A HUNDRED YEARS AGO, William T. Love had big ideas for his housing development called Love Canal. Unfortunately, he ran out of money before the canal was finished and sold the land to Hooker Chemical Corporation. After all, what's the best possible use for a massive canal-shaped pit the length of a hundred football fields? A dump, of course! And what does a chemical corporation need to dump? Toxic chemicals.

By 1953, the canal was full. So Hooker Chemical Corporation poured some dirt over the top, patted it down, and sold the site to... the local school board. In 1955, the 99th Street School welcomed its first 400 students and sent them out to play soccer on the school fields... right above 20,000 tons of toxic waste.

Meanwhile, new homes were built around the school, where residents sipped the chemicals that had seeped into the water supply with their morning coffee. And people began to wonder... why were their kids getting sick? And what were those rusty barrels they found when they dug in their backyards? When they found out that they'd bought land above a chemical dump, and no one had thought to mention this dump before... well, they put on their boxing gloves.

In 1978, a mother named Lois Gibbs founded the Love Canal Parents Movement, which eventually became the Love Canal Homeowners Association. Through research, protests, letter writing campaigns, and more protests, that group eventually forced the government of New York to close the school, buy the neighborhood houses, and relocate the people to safer ground. Most of the old houses were demolished. The solution didn't reverse the birth defects and cancers already experienced by some Love Canal residents, but at least no new residents were exposed.

Foul Fact

When she first learned about the toxic waste dump, Lois Gibbs asked the school board to move her son to a different school. The school board said: No way. If we move one child out of the cesspool, they'll all want to go!

QUESTION 37

Who needs eggs, anyway?

IN 1939, A SWISS SCIENTIST NAMED PAUL MÜLLER created a new pesticide that was highly effective in killing bugs. Its very long chemical formula was quickly reduced to the simple name DDT. Four years later, a typhus epidemic was raging in Naples, Italy. Health officials doused everyone with clouds of the poison, killing the disease-carrying lice. The epidemic ended, and everyone hailed the new chemical as a miracle cure. Müller was awarded the Nobel Prize for Medicine.

While direct exposure to DDT seemed to have little effect on human health, decades later, scientists discovered that DDT had a different kind of dark side. In the 1960s, they learned two new words. *Bioaccumulation* meant that animals collected the poison in their bodies. *Biomagnification* meant that the poison could accumulate across the food chain, so when big animals ate smaller animals, they stored more of the poison, magnifying the problem. If one big bird ate 25 little fish, its body stored 25 times the DDT.

Unfortunately, scientists didn't figure this out until cotton growers had doused their crops with DDT by plane and all of North America had dumped DDT into swamps and bogs to control malaria-carrying mosquitoes. Fish died, and bird eggs grew so brittle that no chicks hatched. Eagle populations plummeted. In some areas, robins completely disappeared.

DDT has been banned in many countries since the 1970s.

Foul Fact

Care for some DDT on your breakfast cereal? Volunteers have eaten small pellets every day for a year to prove that it's safe for humans. Delicious and nutritious? Maybe not. Mice exposed to DDT suffer from reproductive problems, which scientists say may affect human mothers, as well. DDT is also considered a possible cause of cancer, because some animals develop liver tumors when exposed to the chemical.

☠

QUESTION 38

If your cat jumped off a cliff, would you?

IMAGINE YOU LIVE in a fishing village on the shores of Minamata Bay, Japan. For generations, your family has eaten a diet based on seafood. But there's a secret lurking at the bottom of your particular bay: the mud down there is a mercury-laced sludge, courtesy of the local chemical plant.

Your first clue that something's wrong? Your cat goes crazy. So do all the other cats in the neighborhood. Some even throw themselves into the sea. Next, other animals start to have convulsions. And soon after that, children lose the ability to speak, miscarriages increase, and old people

get sick. Doctors diagnose "Minamata disease," which turns out to be a fancy way of saying severe mercury poisoning.

There's one part of this story that's even crazier than the seagoing cats. It's the timeline. Minamata disease was diagnosed in 1956. Researchers discovered massive mercury doses in the fish population by 1959. More than 10,000 people were poisoned. But the government didn't ban fishing in Minamata Bay until nine years later, in 1968.

Why? No one wanted to talk about Minamata Bay. Not the government. Not the chemical company. And not even the people who lived there. The reasons for their silence were both political and cultural.

SILENCE, EVERYONE!

Government Official
"Minamata Bay? Never heard of it!"

Chisso Corporation
"No comment."

Don't complain, or they'll close the factory.

Groom
"Don't mention the disease, or no one will marry me."

Grandma
"If they find out Grandpa's sick, our family will be shamed."

Businesswoman
"They think Minamata people are polluted. No one will hire me."

When did Mom join the WHO?

DIOXINS ARE SOME OF THE NASTIEST POISONS AROUND. They cause cancer. They accumulate in the food chain. And they hang around for years, stored in human and animal fat cells.

The worst part? Dioxins are almost always created by human activity. They're made during industrial processes, or when burning garbage. They're produced by smelters, pump mills, and chemical plants. In 1976, a gas explosion at a chemical plant in Seveso, Italy, exposed thousands of people to dioxin. Those people are still being studied, and even their children are being monitored for possible effects.

According to the World Health Organization, there are three things that can save us from dioxin poisoning:

• Don't let companies produce dioxin in the first place.

• Monitor food products for dioxin.

• Eat a balanced diet.

Eat your greens!

WHO

Eat a balanced diet? Apparently, our mothers have been nagging the World Heath Organization! They say a balanced diet protects people from poisoning because of its variety. If a batch of milk is accidentally contaminated with dioxin, and you live entirely on pizza and chocolate milk, your exposure will be higher. Someone who eats a variety of foods will be better protected.

So, the truth is out. Our mothers and the WHO are conspiring to make us eat our broccoli.

Foul Fact

The Great Lakes that stretch between Canada and the United States contain more than 20 percent of the Earth's fresh water—and 362 added chemicals. Years of industrial dumping, agricultural runoff, and sewage have left the lakes in dire need of environmental care.

☠ QUESTION 40

How do you wage war in the jungle?

REMOVE THE LEAVES ON TREES, OF COURSE.

Between 1962 and 1971, during the Vietnam War, that's what the United States military tried to do. They doused the country with a herbicide called Agent Orange, which made broad-leafed plants lose their leaves. They used more than 50 million liters—enough to fill 20 Olympic-sized swimming pools—and historians estimate that one-fifth of the country's jungles were sprayed.

Agent Orange didn't win the war. What it did was kill thousands of people and cause thousands more miscarriages, cancers, and birth defects, both in Vietnam residents and in soldiers who fought in affected areas. It turns out that Agent Orange contained dioxin. Scientists now think it might cause more than 120 different diseases in humans.

In 1991, the United States government compensated some of the veterans affected by the herbicide. So far, no compensation has been given to Vietnamese victims.

Foul Fact

Agent Orange isn't orange. It was named for the colored bands used on the shipping barrels. Other chemicals used in Vietnam included agents pink, blue, purple, and green—a rainbow's worth of poison.

THE SOLDIERS' SYNDROME

In the years after the 1991 Gulf War in the Middle East, many American soldiers experienced strange symptoms, from migraines to memory problems. Some even developed diseases such as brain cancer and multiple sclerosis. They blamed their illnesses on exposure to poisons used during the war: chemical weapons, smoke from oil well fires, and experimental medications and vaccines.

In 2008, after years of denial by the military, an American congressional committee confirmed that Gulf War Syndrome was real. Although doctors still don't know exactly what caused the syndrome, many veterans have received money to compensate them for their illnesses.

He's fine.

Can an atom a day keep the doctor away?

How come they're bright green and glowing?

IN 1896, A FRENCH SCIENTIST named Antoine Henri Becquerel stuffed some photographic plates in a dark drawer, near a chunk of uranium. When he later retrieved them, the plates had been partially developed! Because he'd already studied X-Rays, Becquerel guessed that the uranium must have emitted rays of energy, without help from any outside source.

By the early 1900s, people understood that elements such as uranium and radium are radioactive, meaning that they give off particles and energy. Many thought this was a good thing and that absorbing the extra particles might be beneficial to humans. For example, everyone knew drinking spring water was good for you. After discovering that water from some underground springs contained small amounts of a radioactive gas called radon, they concluded that more radioactivity would be more beneficial.

One company marketed a new product called the Radium Ore Revigator—it was a large ceramic jar coated with radioactive uranium and used to store drinking water. The company advertised that the Radium Ore Revigator would ease your arthritis pains, help you think more clearly, and even keep your farting under control.

Thousands of American families bought the Revigator. Because illnesses and deaths weren't tracked then the way they are today, researchers can't tell whether the jug killed people. But by the 1930s, scientists had learned that radiation had a dangerous effect on human cells, and swigging from a crock of uranium could eventually cause cancer.

For years, the residents of Tayamo Prefecture in Japan suffered from a strange ailment called *itai-itai,* or ouch-ouch disease. Meanwhile, residents of Niigata, Japan, suffered from mercury poisoning. Neither of these cities is on Minamata Bay, but their illnesses caused a ban on fishing in the mercury-clogged water. How were the three connected?

The Clues:

1. In the 1960s, doctors classified *itai-itai* as a central nervous system disorder. It caused convulsions, miscarriages, and excruciating pain.
2. The bodies of those with *itai-itai* were shown to have high levels of cadmium.
3. In Niigata, Japan, people began to suffer from mercury poisoning— a second outbreak of Minamata disease.
4. Niigata sits along the Agano River, near a chemical plant.
5. Victims from Tayamo Prefecture visited victims in Niigata. Then they visited victims in Minamata Bay and discovered similar problems.
6. One of the affected families sued a local chemical plant. A community organization and a labor union both joined in the movement, demanding money and treatment for people who had been poisoned.

What happened?

Answer:

To ignore the mercury in Minamata Bay, the government needed to keep the problem quiet. But as people compared notes and learned that industrial waste was polluting other waterways and harming more people, they were no longer willing to stay silent. They wanted the government to act, to clean up the rivers and bays and to protect the health of local residents.

Faced with pressure from the family lawsuit, the community organization, and the labor union, the government finally admitted that some of Japan's waterways were poisoned. They banned fishing in Minamata Bay, and even installed a net across the mouth of the bay to keep contaminated fish inside until years had passed and mercury levels had dropped. The net remained in place until 1997.

☠ Chapter 8

POISON POSITIVE

Some of history's most vile poisons were launched on the world in well-intentioned attempts to help society. Before it killed thousands of birds, DDT helped prevent typhus and malaria. The chemical Zyklon B used in the Nazi death camps was originally intended to help farmers raise pest-free crops. These cases just go to show that toxins, used wisely, might be a force for good. In the wrong places or in the wrong hands, though, they can wreak havoc.

In what other ways might poisons, used in careful amounts, actually help humanity? Can venoms be used to communicate with God or heal disease? Believers and researchers are still looking for the answers.

No, you can't text
Great-Aunt Mabel.

How do you talk to spirits?

IN TRADITIONAL CULTURES around the world, shamans and healers have used controlled doses of toxic plants in their rituals and ceremonies. Often, these poisons prompted hallucinations and trance states. People believed they allowed more direct communication with gods or spirits.

- In the Amazon region, people use an extract from a rainforest vine to free the soul from the body, allowing people to enter the spirit world.

- In Siberia, traditional shamans eat small amounts of a poisonous mushroom to gain psychic abilities and healing powers.

- The famous Delphic oracles of ancient Greece may have inhaled the fumes of boiling jimsonweed to prompt their visions of the future.

- About 1700 years ago, Mayan shamans induced trances with poisonous enemas. They injected their rear ends with a concoction of mead, tobacco juice, mushrooms, and morning glory.

THE SERPENT'S BITE

In 1910, a Tennessee preacher named George W. Hensley decided that if the Bible were true, then God would protect his followers from snakebite, as promised in the Gospel of Mark ("And these signs shall follow them that believe: In my name … they shall take up serpents; and if they drink any deadly thing, it shall not hurt them."). George began handling poisonous snakes during his sermons. Over the next few decades, the practice grew more widespread. And in many Pentecostal Holiness churches across the United States and Canada, services include venomous snakes. Some people have even taken strychnine to prove their God-given immunity to poison.

Occasionally, someone is poisoned. There have been about 75 snakebite-related deaths since the movement began. Believers say that God allows the bites to punish wrongdoing, to prove to others that the snakes are deadly, to test the faith of the people, and to show the healing power of faith.

George himself died from a snakebite in 1955, after he refused medical treatment. He was 75 years old.

... and you will be protected!

Eyes to die for!

Does this venom match my eyes?

NEFERTITI, THE EGYPTIAN QUEEN, was the supermodel of the 14th century BC. Her name meant "the beauty has come" and her almond eyes were legendary in the Mediterranean. She outlined them with kohl, called *mesdemet* by the Egyptians. Although the dark powder contained both lead compounds and chlorine, Nefertiti didn't know she was painting herself with poison.

She wasn't the last woman to use potentially toxic makeup, unaware of the danger. In ancient Greece, people used white lead as face paint. Women in 18th-century Europe used a mercury compound to cover their pimples. Victorian-age ladies rinsed their eyes with belladonna—deadly nightshade—to get the somewhat-ill-with-tuberculosis look that was all the rage at the time.

And some poisons are still being used in makeup today. One company claims that its synthetic snake venom smooths the skin. Another company's moisturizer contains a protein copied from viper venom, said to diminish wrinkles—for $450 a bottle.

Snake oil or miracle cure?

STEP RIGHT UP! Take a little tonic for that cough or a sip of syrup for your aches. Are you trying to cure your child's teething pain? Have we got the solution for you! Our soothing syrup—just a touch of morphine added—will put your baby right to sleep. And if you're hoping to kick your drinking habit, try our patent medicine. At 40 percent alcohol, it'll help you right along.

These were some of the claims made by North American salespeople in the late 1800s, when bottled cures were so popular—and so unsuccessful—they became known as snake oil. That name comes from a traditional Chinese arthritis treatment, which actually is made from snake extracts. But while the original snake oil might have been effective, the term quickly came to mean "fake cure" in North America. Some 19th-century concoctions included heroin, arsenic, even petroleum. They probably didn't kill patients, but they weren't too likely to cure them, either.

step right up!

And fall right down.

Foul Fact

The Food and Drug Administration (FDA) was created in the United States in 1906. Six years later, its role was expanded and it was told to make sure dangerous cures and fake medicines weren't sold to American buyers.

It's new and improved.

You mean it won't kill me?

CURE-ALL

QUESTION 45

Can poison cure poison?

ACCORDING TO HOMEOPATHS, who practice a form of what many people believe to be an alternative medicine, all you need to cure a poisoned patient is a minute amount of the poison that made him ill in the first place. You dilute that sample in water, again and again, shaking it between each dilution. Then, when none of the original poison remains but the water molecules still retain a "memory" of it, the remedy is complete.

Invented by a German doctor named Samuel Hahnemann in the late 1700s, homeopathy is based on a principle called the "law of similars." Experimenting with the malaria treatments of his time, Samuel decided that the most effective drugs mimicked the symptoms of the illness itself. Therefore, any valid malaria treatment should cause fevers and chills. And a lead poisoning treatment should include lead.

The science of homeopathy has been debunked by countless studies. Modern researchers are vehemently clear that water cannot "remember" poison that it once encountered. They say that in the 1700s, when so many common medicines were actually harmful, the benign properties of homeopathic dilutions were an improvement. Obviously, someone drinking nontoxic dilutions would feel better than someone sipping mercury. But now that Western medicine has improved, patients cured by homeopathy are simply experiencing a comforting placebo effect—they think they're cured, so they feel better.

Still, despite the critics, many people feel that they benefit from homeopathic treatments, and homeopathy continues to draw followers around the world.

QUESTION 48

Is toad venom like snake oil?

were entirely wrong about most of their products. But that doesn't mean all early medications were useless. In fact, Western scientists are "rediscovering" some ancient Asian cures, and finding that their poisonous qualities have just the right bite.

In China, a medicine called *hauchansu* is made from toad venom. It's been used to treat cancerous growths for centuries. In the 1970s, researchers in China began clinical tests on the substance. They found that 16 percent of lung cancer patients improved significantly when dosed with the poison.

American doctors began their own research in 2003, using up to eight times the traditional Chinese dose. In many patients, cancer growth temporarily stopped. In one, the cancer shrank—a sign that maybe toad venom isn't the same as snake oil, after all?

Venom hasn't done a lot for me personally.

Don't be a chicken. It's good for you.

STING OPERATION

Doctors sometimes use bee venom to desensitize people with allergies. So far, that's the venom's only common use. But researchers in Eastern Europe and Asia are testing it as a treatment for arthritis, rheumatism, epilepsy, and even multiple sclerosis.

QUESTION 47

Can Gila monsters cure diabetes?

SCIENTISTS ARE STUDYING all sorts of venomous creatures, looking for ways they can be used to help humans. Here are some of their results:

- The venom of the Russell's viper causes blood to thicken. It's used to treat hemophiliacs—people whose blood doesn't clot properly. The venom is now also used to test for a rare blood disorder while babies are still in the womb.

- Captopril is a drug used around the world to treat high blood pressure. The substance was discovered in the venom of a lancehead snake from South America.

- A drug called bryostatin was first found in colonies of tiny creatures that live on the hulls of ocean liners and emit a toxic substance to protect their larvae. Synthetic forms of bryostatin are being tested for use in treating cancer, depression, and memory loss.

- Exenatide, a drug used to treat diabetes, was discovered in the venom of the Gila monster.

Ow!

FANG AND FORTUNE

Snake venoms are particularly complicated mixtures of proteins and other molecules—different according to the species, the region, and even the age of the snake. Researchers have spent years testing different extracts for medical use. In Australia, scientists have found a compound that damages the lining of the blood vessels that feed cancerous tumors. In the United States, an extract from copperhead venom has been shown to stop tumor growth. And an extract from the Malayan pit viper may help restore blood flow to the brain after a stroke.

$100

Does that tree come in pill form?

INSTRUCTIONS FOR CURING MALARIA:

1. Write a secret phrase on a piece of paper.
2. Tie the paper to a young girl, using a particularly long string.
3. Recite prayers about the Holy Trinity.

Hopefully, the prayers worked. The other parts of this early malaria treatment wouldn't have done much, except maybe annoy young girls. But in the 1600s, people around the world were desperate for a cure.

Enter the traditional healers of Peru, who knew that something in the bark of the cinchona tree could ease the shivering induced by high fevers. A Jesuit missionary in the region heard about the treatment and shipped some bark back to Europe to help treat malaria cases. The substance became known as quinine.

Quinine is poisonous. It causes symptoms ranging from ringing in the ears and headaches to vomiting and death. But in small doses, it was the best method available for preventing and controlling malaria. Cinchona tree plantations soon sprang up in India, Costa Rica, the Philippines, Indonesia, and Africa. Quinine remained the primary treatment for malaria until the 1940s, and is still used in some cases today.

Oh yesh, I'm guarding againsht malaria... hic!

And quinine is only one of the drugs based on poisonous plant extracts. There are well over 100 of them, from heart medications to painkillers.

Foul Fact

In the 1700s, when British colonists sat on their tropical verandas sipping gin and tonics, they were having a good time—and boosting their malaria medication. Tonic water contains small amounts of quinine.

SPRINTING FOR STRYCHNINE

Can poison improve human performance? Not ethically… at least not these days. But a century ago, the rules weren't so clear.

Three-quarters of the way through the 1904 Olympic marathon in St. Louis, Missouri, runner Thomas J. Hicks was out of energy. His trainer came to the rescue—with a dose of strychnine. Although larger doses of that plant poison can cause fatal seizures, small doses act as a stimulant. Eager for Hicks's leg muscles to start churning once again, the trainer gave him a strychnine pill and a brimming glass of brandy, and, later, another strychnine dose.

FAST!   FASTER!   FASTEST!

Fortunately, Hicks made it over the finish line before he collapsed. (Today's doctors say a third dose of the poison would have killed him.) He placed second in the race. Then, when it turned out that the first-place winner had hitched a ride in his trainer's car for part of the route, Hicks was awarded the gold medal. Strychnine for the win!

I'm not that crazy about bringing back DDT.

Did we ditch DDT too soon?

IN THE 1970s, when songbirds were suffering and eagles were nearing extinction, the world moved quickly to ban the use of DDT. But today, some scientists argue that if we used it cautiously, it could help fight malaria in developing countries.

Carried by mosquitoes, malaria kills more than 2.5 million people a year. The mosquito-killing alternatives to DDT are expensive, and sometimes twice as nasty to humans. DDT supporters say that saving human lives should be more important than whether or not the pesticide harms wildlife.

So, will the ban last? Some countries, including India, have returned to spraying DDT over large areas. Other countries depend on systems of insecticide-coated mosquito nets and a combination of other poisons—effective, but more expensive.

Not even international health organizations can agree on which method is best. And until the world decides how to prevent and treat malaria... don't count your eagles before they're hatched.

Foul Fact

In the 1950s, the use of DDT almost eradicated bedbugs in industrialized nations. Today, the bugs are back! Outbreaks have plagued New York City retail stores, Canadian universities, New Zealand hotels, and homes around the world.

Racing to His Doom

In the 1930s, Phar Lap was a celebrated Australian race horse. He won 37 races in Australia before his owners shipped him to the United States. After winning a single race in California, Phar Lap collapsed and died. For years, Australian fans were convinced that American gangsters had poisoned the animal. But when the horse trainer's diary was found in 2008, it revealed something different.

The Clues:

1. An autopsy showed that Phar Lap's stomach and intestines were red and swollen.
2. To keep him performing at his best, the trainer used a wide variety of tonics and ointments.
3. One of the main tonics was laced with arsenic.
4. At the time, it was common to give racehorses stimulants to help them run.

Can you guess how Phar Lap died?

Answer: If given enough tonic, Phar Lap could have been killed by the arsenic alone. But strychnine was also a common stimulant given that day—the same stimulant given to 1910 marathon runner Thomas J. Hicks. When the trainer's diaries were found, they revealed the use of arsenic, strychnine, belladonna, caffeine, and even cocaine. These poisons gave Phar Lap some extra speed—and sped him to his death.

Friends?

THE LAST GASP

DO WE RUN FROM EVERY VENOMOUS CREATURE, or study them for possible cancer cures? Do we douse our homes with insecticides, or let that brown recluse spider keep his hidden corner? And how do we balance the needs of industry with the needs of wildlife?

Millions of years after people encountered the first venomous plants and animals, and hundreds of years after we began using toxins in manu-facturing, we still aren't sure how to answer these questions.

What hunts humans?

FROM COBRAS AND KRAITS to stingrays and scorpions, hundreds of creatures are capable of killing us. Even tiny frogs, bright and shiny as gemstones, can be lethal if handled. Knowing this, is it safe to leave the house? What's lurking around the corner, waiting to pounce?

Nothing.

In the entire world, there is not a single venomous creature intentionally hunting humans. Animals have developed toxins for two reasons: to immobilize their prey and to protect themselves. Even for the largest poisonous snakes and lizards, a person is too big to swallow. We're not prey. It's only if we seem to pose a threat that we might be bitten.

People know this, but they still fear poisonous creatures. And kill them. Every spring, hunters descend on the American south for rattlesnake roundups. As part of multiday festivals, they kill thousands of snakes, sometimes by beheading them and sometimes by pouring gasoline on dens and setting them on fire. Other snakes are captured and used in live shows. According to the Humane Society, the rattlesnake is one of the most exploited creatures on the continent.

So... who's hunting whom?

I'm only trying to survive.

PEACE PACT

Long after King Mithridates searched for the perfect antidote, there's still no such thing as a miracle cure for poison. But, really… we probably don't need one. Instead, we need to keep industrial poisons in check, stay away from gas-belching lakes, and sign a Mutual Avoidance Treaty with the venomous animals of the world.

AGREEMENT

between Party A
(henceforth to be known as "the people")

and Party B
(henceforth to be known as "the snakes"):

You don't bother us.

We won't bother you.

Further Reading

Backshall, Steve. *Venomous Animals of the World*. Baltimore: Johns
Hopkins University Press, 2007.

Dewey, Jennifer Owings. *Poison Dart Frogs*. Honesdale, PA: Boyds Mills
Press, 1998.

Ricciuti, Edward R. *Killer Animals*. Guildford, CT: Lyons Press, 2003.

———. *Killer Seas*. Guildford, CT: Lyons Press, 2003.

Singer, Marilyn. *Venom*. Plain City, OH: Darby Creek Publishing, 2007.

Stewart, Amy. *Wicked Plants*. Chapel Hill, NC: Algonquin Books, 2009.

Stone, Lynn M. *Snakes with Venom*. Vero Beach, FL: Rourke Book, 2001.

Bibliography

Bayliss, Richard. "Sir John Franklin's Last Arctic Expedition." *Journal of the Royal Society of Medicine*. March 2002: 151–53.

Davis, Wade. "Medicine Man." *The Geographical Magazine*. June 1997: 44–47.

"DDT—A Brief History and Status." Environmental Protection Agency website. www.epa.gov/pesticides/factsheets/chemicals/ddt-brief-history-status.htm.

"Dioxins and Their Effects on Human Health." World Health Organization website. www.who.int/mediacentre/factsheets/fs225/en/index.html.

Emsley, John. *The Elements of Murder*. Oxford: Oxford University Press, 2005.

"Experts Dispute '84 Probe into Baby Deaths at Sick Kids." *Toronto Star*. Oct. 12, 1995: A16.

"Facts about Sarin." Centers for Disease Control and Prevention website. www.bt.cdc.gov/agent/sarin/basics/facts.asp.

Fields, Scott. "Great Lakes: Resource at Risk." *Environmental Health Perspectives*. March 2005.

Flores, Graciela. "How to Harvest a Harvester." *Natural History*. Dec. 2008/Jan. 2009: 10.

"Garter Snakes Dangerous?" *Boca Raton News*. Nov. 18, 1975: 3.

Gibbs, Lois Marie. "History: Love Canal: The Start of a Movement." Boston University website. www.bu.edu/lovecanal/canal/index.html.

Goldfrank, Lewis R. et al. *Goldfrank's Toxicologic Emergencies*. New York: McGraw-Hill, 2006.

Hall, Harriet. "Homeopathy." *Skeptic*. Jan. 2009: 8–9.

Hertsgaard, Mark. "Bhopal's Legacy." *The Nation*. May 24, 2004: 6–7.

Holloway, Marguerite. "The Killing Lakes." *Scientific American*. July 2000: 92–99.

"How Volcanoes Work." San Diego State University website. www.geology.sdsu.edu/how_volcanoes_work/Volcanic_gases.html.

"Howl from the Bowel." *Discover*. Oct. 1995: 25.

Karliner, Joshue, Alba Morales, and Dara O'Rourke. "The Barons of Bromide." *The Ecologist*. May/June 1997: 90–98.

Kettles, Nick. "A Nasty Taste in the Mouth." *The Ecologist*. May 2008: 46–50.

Kinley, David H. "Poisoned Water." *World Watch*. Jan./Feb. 2003: 22–27.

Kunzig, Robert. "Style of the Nile." *Discover*. Sept. 1999: 80–83.

MacInnis, Peter. *Poisons*. New York: Arcade Publishing, 2004.

MacKenzie, Debora. "Fresh Evidence on Bhopal Disaster." *New Scientist*. Dec. 7, 2002: 6–7.

Newbery, Lillian. "Sick Kids' Called Slow to Realize Deaths Were Deliberate." *Toronto Star*. Aug. 23, 1985: A7.

Newman, Cathy. "Zyklon B and the Camp of Death." *National Geographic*. May 2005: 22–25.

Pain, Stephanie. "From Poison to Plague: Mithridates's Marvelous Medicine." *New Scientist*. Jan. 26, 2008: 52–53.

"Picnic Pests or Ecological Marvels?" *USA Today Magazine*. July 2004: 46–52.

Reutter, Sharon. "Hazards of Chemical Weapons Release during War: New Perspectives." *Environmental Health Perspectives*. Dec. 1999: 985–90.

Spinney, Laura. "The Killer Bean of Calabar." *New Scientist*. June 28, 2003: 178.

Stewart, Amy. *Wicked Plants*. Chapel Hill, NC: Algonquin Books, 2009.

Tennesen, Michael. "Going Head-to-Head with Killer Bees." *National Wildlife*. Feb./March 2001: 16–17.

"The Death of Sir Alexander Ogston." *The Canadian Medical Association Journal*. April 1929: 412.

Timbrell, John. *The Poison Paradox*. Oxford: Oxford University Press, 2005.

Waltner-Toews, David. *Food, Sex, Salmonella*. Vancouver: Greystone Books, 2008.

Index

Franklin, Sir John 41
frogs 4, 9, 101
    golden dart frog 8
fugu 14
funnel-web spider 17
furans 54

garbage 54, 81
garter snake 15
gas chambers 70
Geneva Convention 56
Germany 55–56, 57
giant centipede 18
Gibbs, Lois 76
Gila monster 95
golden dart frog 8
goliath bird-eating spider
    17
Great Lakes 82
Greece 28, 36, 88, 90
Greenland 39
Greenpeace 74
Gulf War Syndrome 84
Guyana 69

Haber, Fritz 70
Hahnemann, Samuel 92
Harley, John 65
harvester ant 24
hatters 38
Hawaii 52–53
heart rate 27, 71
hellebore 28
hemlock 32, 61, 62, 65
henbane 62
Hensley, George W. 89
heroin 91
Hicks, Thomas J. 97
Hitler, Adolf 70
homeopathy 92

Hooker Chemical
    Corporation 75–76
horned lizard 24
Humane Society 101
hunting 8
Hussein, Saddam 58
hydrogen peroxide 23
hydroquinone 23

incinerators 54, 81
India 73–74
Indian Ocean 5
Indonesia 10
inland taipan 5
insulin 68
Iraq 20, 48, 56, 58
itai-itai 86
Italy 56, 76, 81

Japan 14, 56, 59, 78–80, 86
jellyfish 13
jimsonweed 27, 28, 88
Jones, Jim 69
Jonestown 69

Kenya 32
Kerr, Warwick 20
killer bees 20–21
King Charles II 37
King Mithridates 62–63,
    102
Kirrha 28
komodo dragon 10
krait 7, 101

Lake Nyos 51
lancehead snake 95
laze 52–53

lead 41, 42, 90
    in cosmetics 90
    in paint 42–43
    in toys 43
lizards 10
    horned lizard 24
    komodo dragon 10
Love Canal 75–76
Love, William T. 75–76

Mad Hatter 38
makeup *see* cosmetics
malaria 92, 96, 98
Malayan pit viper 95
Malaysia 31
manchineel tree 31
mandrake root 27
Markov, Georgi 71
Masai 32
Mayan shamans 88
medicine 12, 19, 32
    medical treatment
        for poisoning 62–63
    medical treatment
        with poisons 35, 40,
        64–65, 67, 68, 91–96
    see also antivenin,
    vaccines
mercury 36, 37, 38–39, 40,
    42, 48, 49, 74, 78–79, 86
methyl mercury 48
Minamata Disease 78–80,
    86
Mithridates *see* King
    Mithridates
morphine 91
Müller, Paul 76
murders 66–67, 68, 69,
    70, 71
mushrooms 30, 61, 88
mustard gas 56, 58

About the Author

TANYA LLOYD KYI lives a safe and venom-free life. She has never been stung by a jellyfish, stabbed with an umbrella tip, or doused in pesticides. She prefers french fries to *fugu*.

Tanya has written both fiction and nonfiction for middle grade and young adult readers. Her interests include science and social issues and her 2005 title, *The Blue Jean Book*, won the Christie Harris Illustrated Children's Literature Prize.

Now that Tanya has learned about thallium, ricin, and nightshade berries, she is considering a future in crime writing. Or forensics. Or possibly alchemy. In the meantime, she lives in Vancouver, B.C., with her husband, Min, and their two children.

About the Illustrator

ROSS KINNAIRD has illustrated about a dozen books for children. When asked how he comes up with his ideas, he replies that he sits in a bath of warm lemonade with a frozen chicken on his head!

The thing he enjoys most about being an illustrator is visiting schools to talk about books and drawing funny pictures of teachers. He has been to about 150 schools and spoken to thousands of kids.

He loves to travel and has visited Australia, Israel, Morocco, and countries throughout Asia and Europe.